MR. MARMALADE

BY NOAH HAIDLE

DRAMATISTS
PLAY SERVICE

MR. MARMALADE received its world premiere by South Coast Repertory (David Emmes, Producing Artistic Director; Martin Benson, Artistic Director) in Costa Mesa, California, opening on April 25, 2004. It was directed by Ethan McSweeny; the set design was by Rachel Hauck; the costume design was by Angela Balogh Calin; the lighting design was by Scott Zielinski; the sound design was by Michael Roth; the assistant director was Joshua N. Hsu; the dramaturg was Jerry Patch; the production manager was Tom Aberger; and the stage manager was Jamie A. Tucker. The cast was as follows:

LUCY .... Eliza Pryor Nagel
MR. MARMALADE .... Glenn Fleshier
SOOKIE, SUNFLOWER .... Heidi Dippold
BRADLEY .... Marc Vietor
EMILY .... Heidi Dippold
GEORGE, CACTUS, A MAN .... Larry Bates
LARRY .... Guilford Adams

MR. MARMALADE was originally produced in New York City by Roundabout Theatre Company (Todd Haimes, Artistic Director), opening on November 20, 2005. It was directed by Michael Greif; the set design was by Allen Moyer; the costume design was by Constance Hoffman; the lighting design was by Kevin Adams; the sound design was by Walter Trarbach and Tony Smolenski IV; and the original music was by Michael Friedman. The cast was as follows:

LUCY .... Mamie Gummer
MR. MARMALADE .... Michael C. Hall
SOOKIE, EMILY, A SUNFLOWER .... Virginia Louise Smith
GEORGE, A CACTUS, A MAN .... Michael Chernus
LARRY .... Pablo Schreiber
BRADLEY .... David Costabile

CHARACTERS

LUCY — 4 years old. Has a vivid imagination.

MR. MARMALADE — Her imaginary friend. Dresses nice. Never has any time for her.

SOOKIE — Lucy's mom. Relies on men for more than they're good for.

EMILY — The babysitter. The first girl in her class to get boobs.

GEORGE — Her boyfriend. A jock. Wears a letter jacket.

LARRY — 5 years old. Has bandages on his wrists. The youngest suicide attempt in the history of New Jersey.

BRADLEY — Mr. Marmalade's personal assistant. Can sing like an angel.

A CACTUS and A SUNFLOWER — Talking plants.

A MAN — A one-night stand.

PLACE

A living room in New Jersey.

TIME

Now.

MR. MARMALADE

I.

OF THE STRAINED RELATIONSHIP OF LUCY AND HER IMAGINARY FRIEND MR. MARMALADE

A living room in New Jersey. Let's not get very naturalistic about it. More the suggestion of a room than a room. Lucy is playing with Ken and Barbie. She wears a pink tutu in a state of disrepair. Barbie wears a tutu, too. Mr. Marmalade appears. He's very well dressed. Suit, briefcase, nice shoes.

MR. MARMALADE. Good evening.
LUCY. I thought you weren't coming.
MR. MARMALADE. I carved out some time.
LUCY. Thirty minutes?
MR. MARMALADE. Ten.
LUCY. That's not very many.
MR. MARMALADE. It's the best I could do. Next week will be better. I promise.
LUCY. We'd better get started.
MR. MARMALADE. What is it today?
LUCY. House.
MR. MARMALADE. I see. *(He opens his briefcase and whips out a tea set. Cups, saucers, spoons.)* Whenever you're ready.
LUCY. Come down here. *(He sits.)* Would you like a cup of coffee?
MR. MARMALADE. Have we started?
LUCY. Yes.
MR. MARMALADE. I would love a cup of coffee. *(She pours coffee.)*
LUCY. How do you take it?

MR. MARMALADE. Black. *(She puts sugar in the coffee. Gives him the cup.)* I said black.

LUCY. Did you? I'm sorry. Would you like another cup?

MR. MARMALADE. Yes, please.

LUCY. Oh shoot, we just ran out. Would you like me to brew some more?

MR. MARMALADE. Don't worry about it.

LUCY. Are you sure?

MR. MARMALADE. Are you angry with me, Lucy?

LUCY. Why would I be angry with you, honey?

MR. MARMALADE. Not play angry. Real angry.

LUCY. I'm not angry. I just wish you weren't so busy.

MR. MARMALADE. So do I. I wish I could play with you all night, but work is crazy right now.

LUCY. I know. I'm sorry. We'd better keep going. Not much time.

MR. MARMALADE. Okay.

LUCY. Would you like more coffee?

MR. MARMALADE. I thought we ran out.

LUCY. I have a fresh pot right here. Black?

MR. MARMALADE. Please. *(She pours some coffee. He sips it.)*

LUCY. What do you think?

MR. MARMALADE. Delicious.

LUCY. It's a new blend I had flown in from Peru.

MR. MARMALADE. It's absolutely wonderful, Lucy.

LUCY. I'm so glad you're home from work. You have no idea how lonely this house gets.

MR. MARMALADE. I can only imagine. It's so good to be home.

LUCY. Why don't you touch me anymore?

SOOKIE. *(Offstage.)* Lucy!!!

MR. MARMALADE. What?

LUCY. You haven't touched me in weeks. Is there somebody else?

MR. MARMALADE. What? No. Don't be ridiculous.

LUCY. Someone at work? That new intern?

SOOKIE. *(Offstage.)* Lucy!? What are you doing, Lucy?

LUCY. I'm busy!!! *(To Mr. Marmalade.)* Is there somebody else?

MR. MARMALADE. Of course not. How could you ask me such a thing?

LUCY. You're at the office until the dead of night. And when you are home you barely even look at me, let alone lay a finger on me.

MR. MARMALADE. I'm tired when I get home. I'm exhausted. All I can think of is going to sleep. I barely have the energy to shovel food in my mouth.

LUCY. Excuses, excuses.

MR. MARMALADE. I'm sorry. I'll do better. Cut back at work. We'll take a vacation. Mexico. Cabo San Lucas. First class across the board.

LUCY. Mexico! You promise?

MR. MARMALADE. I promise. *(Sookie enters in a slip and high heels. She carries two dresses.)*

SOOKIE. Which one?

LUCY. Mom, I'm busy.

SOOKIE. What are you doing?

LUCY. Mr. Marmalade just got home from the office and he has to leave in like five minutes so I'd greatly appreciate it if you left us alone.

SOOKIE. Hello, Mr. Marmalade.

MR. MARMALADE. Hello, Mother.

LUCY. He says hello.

SOOKIE. Tell him hello for me too.

MR. MARMALADE. Such a nice woman, your mother.

SOOKIE. Which dress should I wear?

LUCY. I think it's very rude for you to barge in here when I have company. You owe Mr. Marmalade an apology. You know how precious his time is.

SOOKIE. Mr. Marmalade, I'm very sorry.

MR. MARMALADE. It's not a problem at all. I adore the time I spend with your mother.

LUCY. He accepts your apology. Begrudgingly, I might add.

SOOKIE. Maybe Mr. Marmalade has a preference about which dress I wear.

MR. MARMALADE. I prefer the red dress, although I imagine just about anything would look stunning on you.

LUCY. He likes the red one.

SOOKIE. Me too. Thank you, Mr. Marmalade. *(She kisses Lucy on the head and exits.)*

MR. MARMALADE. There's no need to thank me. I'm flattered that she holds my opinion in such high regard.

LUCY. Where were we?

MR. MARMALADE. Mexico.

LUCY. That's right. Cabo San Lucas.

MR. MARMALADE. First class across the board. A huge white bed with ostrich feather pillows. Men in tuxedos holding umbrellas for the sun. Top-shelf margaritas on the hotel veranda watching the sunset.

LUCY. When can we go?

MR. MARMALADE. We'll go next month. Work will lighten up.

LUCY. You promise you're not cheating on me?

MR. MARMALADE. I promise I'm not cheating on you.

LUCY. You pinky swear?

MR. MARMALADE. I pinky swear. *(They pinky swear.)*

LUCY. I knew you weren't. Oh, honey, I'm sorry I accused you of that. I'm alone here all by myself night and day. My imagination runs wild. You have no idea. *(His beeper goes off. It startles him.)*

MR. MARMALADE. Oh shit, my beeper.

LUCY. You're not going to go back to the office tonight, are you, dear?

MR. MARMALADE. Not play beeper. My real beeper.

LUCY. No!!!

MR. MARMALADE. I have to go.

LUCY. You said ten minutes.

MR. MARMALADE. I know I did. But I have to go.

LUCY. When will I see you again?

MR. MARMALADE. Let me check my Blackberry. *(Scrolls through his Blackberry.)* This week is terrible. I might have forty-five minutes on Thursday. Maybe we could do sushi. I'll have Bradley call you.

LUCY. You said we'd do sushi last week.

MR. MARMALADE. I know I did. I'm sorry. *(Kisses her on the head.)* I have to go. Goodbye. *(He disappears.)*

LUCY. Goodbye. *(Sookie enters in the red dress.)*

SOOKIE. What do you think? *(She sashays.)*

LUCY. It's okay.

SOOKIE. What do you think, Mr. Marmalade?

LUCY. He's not here.

SOOKIE. Where is he?

LUCY. At the office. He's a very important man. I can't expect him to spend his whole night here drinking coffee with me.

SOOKIE. Babysitter'll be here in half an hour. Can you hold down the fort until then?

LUCY. Which one is it?

SOOKIE. Emily.

LUCY. Ugggh.

SOOKIE. You like Emily.

LUCY. No I don't. She smells like cigarettes. She only talks about her boyfriend and her breasts coming in.

SOOKIE. Emily is a very nice girl and you're going to have a good time.

LUCY. I don't see the point of having a babysitter at all.

SOOKIE. Lucy, you're four years old.

LUCY. I can take care of myself.

SOOKIE. You're too young to take care of yourself.

LUCY. Who says?

SOOKIE. I say. *(The doorbell rings.)* We'll have to discuss this later. How do I look?

LUCY. Fine.

SOOKIE. Just fine or pretty good?

LUCY. Just fine.

SOOKIE. Thank you for your support, Lucy. *(Kisses her on the head.)* No TV and in bed by nine o'clock. Do you hear me?

LUCY. Yes, ma'am.

SOOKIE. Good night, dear. *(She goes.)*

LUCY. Good night. *(Lucy is alone.)*

II.

OF THE CONVERSATION BETWEEN LUCY AND EMILY THE BABYSITTER, DURING WHICH THEY TALK ABOUT MR. MARMALADE AND HIS DELINQUENT BEHAVIOR AND HOW MEN ARE LIKE THAT IN GENERAL UNLESS YOU KEEP THEM IN LINE

Emily watches TV, eating a big bowl of popcorn. Lucy is talking on a hairbrush like it's a cell phone.

LUCY. *(On phone.)* You're breaking up. No, I can hear you now. Tonight? Nothing. Just hanging out. I've got a babysitter. I know, can you believe it? No. She's okay. Kinda dumb. She smokes cigarettes. Her clothes smell like cigarettes. I know, disgusting, right? Teenagers. It's an awkward time, you're right. She's got a boyfriend. Yeah. I don't know, I'll ask her. *(To Emily.)* Have you had sex with your boyfriend yet?

EMILY. What?

LUCY. *(On phone.)* She's totally avoiding the question. Yeah. I bet she has, too. She doesn't look like a virgin.

EMILY. Who are you talking to?

LUCY. *(On the phone.)* Just a sec. *(To Emily.)* I'm on the phone. Would you mind not interrupting? Thanks. *(On the phone.)* She keeps interrupting. I know? Right? Mind your manners. I will tell her that. You gotta go? Are you sure? Okay. No. I understand. Ciao. *(Hangs up the phone.)*

EMILY. Who were you talking to?

LUCY. No one you know.

EMILY. Was it Mr. Marmalade?

LUCY. How do you know Mr. Marmalade?

EMILY. We hang out all the time.

LUCY. You do not!

EMILY. We go to the mall and get our nails done.

LUCY. Mr. Marmalade does not get his nails done!!!

EMILY. Chill out. We don't go to the mall. Your Mom told me about him.

LUCY. What'd she say?

EMILY. Says he's a deadbeat.

LUCY. He's very busy. He's a very important man.

EMILY. Don't matter how important he is. He's gotta make time for you.

LUCY. He wants to make more time for me. Things are just so crazy at the office right now.

EMILY. My boyfriend George used to say he was too busy to hang out with me.

LUCY. What'd you do?

EMILY. I stopped hooking up with him.

LUCY. Then did he have more time for you?

EMILY. You better believe he did.

LUCY. That's what I'll do.

EMILY. Do you even hook up with Mr. Marmalade?

LUCY. I think I do.

EMILY. Either you do or you don't.

LUCY. Then I do.

EMILY. Let me talk to him.

LUCY. He's in a meeting.

EMILY. Gimme the phone.

LUCY. No.

EMILY. Fine. I've got my own phone. *(She dials her real cell phone.)*

LUCY. You don't even know his number.

EMILY. Hello? Mr. Marmalade? It's Emily. Hey, what's up?

LUCY. You're not taking to him.

EMILY. No, she's right here. I know, she gets pretty annoying, doesn't she?

LUCY. That's not him!!!

EMILY. She totally has a crush on you. *(Lucy is grabbing for the phone.)*

LUCY. Shut up!!! I do not!

EMILY. She wants to marry you and have your babies!

LUCY. I do not! *(Lucy grabs the cell phone.)* Hello? Mr. Marmalade? Mr. Marmalade?

EMILY. He must have hung up.

LUCY. You weren't talking to him.

EMILY. I totally was.

LUCY. NO YOU WEREN'T!

EMILY. Okay. Chill out. I wasn't talking to Mr. Marmalade. Jesus.

LUCY. You don't even know him.

EMILY. I've never met him, okay?

LUCY. Okay.

EMILY. Jealousy is not attractive to men, Lucy. Trust me. *(Silence.)*

LUCY. Let's play Tea Party.

EMILY. I want to watch TV.

LUCY. I want to play Tea Party.

EMILY. My show's on.

LUCY. It's on commercial.

EMILY. So I'm watching the commercial.

LUCY. What do you think my mom is paying you for? I want a Tea Party.

EMILY. All right, all right.

LUCY. Come down here. *(She sits on the ground.)*

LUCY. What kind of tea would you like?

EMILY. What kind do you have?

LUCY. Earl Grey, English Breakfast, Green Tea, Darjeeling Oolong.

EMILY. I don't know. Which one is good?

LUCY. I prefer Darjeeling Oolong.

EMILY. I'll have the English Breakfast.

LUCY. Which is also excellent. *(She pours imaginary water. Puts in an imaginary tea bag.)* How would you like it? I take mine with sugar and milk.

EMILY. That sounds pretty good.

LUCY. Wonderful. *(She adds sugar and milk. Hands it to Emily, who tentatively sips.)* Well?

EMILY. It's good.

LUCY. Not too sweet?

EMILY. No, it's really good. Listen, I'm gonna go outside for a few minutes.

LUCY. But it's a tea party. *(Emily chugs the rest of her imaginary tea.)*

EMILY. I finished my tea.

LUCY. But I made cucumber sandwiches.

EMILY. I'm sorry. I'm not very good at make-believe.

LUCY. You're going to smoke a cigarette.

EMILY. I like a cigarette after a cup of tea. Why don't you invite Mr. Marmalade to your tea party?

LUCY. He's busy.

EMILY. I'll be back in a few minutes, okay?

LUCY. Fine. *(Emily leaves. Bradley appears, unseen by Lucy. He's dressed exactly like Mr. Marmalade. Nice suit. Shoes. Briefcase. He also wears big wraparound sunglasses.)*

BRADLEY. Lucy.

LUCY. Oh, you scared me, Bradley.

BRADLEY. Sorry. *(They kiss on the cheek. Very adult-like.)*

LUCY. What are you doing here? I wasn't expecting to hear from you until the first of the week.

BRADLEY. The schedule has changed. Mr. M was hoping you would be free this weekend.

LUCY. I'm free.

BRADLEY. Excellent. I'll pencil you in for brunch on Sunday.

LUCY. I was just sitting down for tea, would you like some?

BRADLEY. That would be delightful. Do you happen to have Darjeeling Oolong?

LUCY. Of course. *(Bradley sits. She pours the tea.)* I'm afraid I'm fresh out of milk.

BRADLEY. No problem. I've got some. *(He opens his briefcase and takes out some milk. He pours it.)*

LUCY. Thank you, Bradley.

BRADLEY. Are those cucumber sandwiches?

LUCY. Would you like one?

BRADLEY. Yes, please. *(He takes one. Eats.)* Nothing compliments a cup of tea like a cucumber sandwich.

LUCY. I know what you mean.

BRADLEY. What time would be convenient for you on Sunday?

LUCY. Anytime would be fine. Why are you wearing sunglasses?

BRADLEY. Because UV rays are bad for your eyes. Haven't you heard?

LUCY. It's dark out, Bradley.

BRADLEY. What time on Sunday?

LUCY. Noon.

BRADLEY. *(Writing.)* Sunday. Noon. Brunch with Lucy. Got it. Thank you for the tea and the cucumber sandwich, but I'd better get back to the office. *(She grabs Bradley's sunglasses. Bradley's got a big fat shiner under his right eye.)*

LUCY. Oh my God.

BRADLEY. It's nothing.

LUCY. Did he do this?

BRADLEY. I fell down some stairs.

LUCY. Bradley, did Mr. Marmalade hit you?

BRADLEY. It was an accident. He didn't really mean to hit me.

LUCY. Why did he hit you?

BRADLEY. It was my fault. I forgot to pick up his dry cleaning, when I knew he had a very important dinner with a client. I knew he needed his gray suit. I forgot to pick it up. It was all my fault.

LUCY. He hit you over the drycleaning.

BRADLEY. He's under so much pressure. You have no idea.

LUCY. That's no excuse.

BRADLEY. You're not going to tell anyone, are you?

LUCY. I think I should.

BRADLEY. No! You have to promise me you won't. Lucy, I can't lose this job.

LUCY. There are things more important than your job, Bradley.

BRADLEY. Please, Lucy. I'm begging you. Please don't tell anyone.

LUCY. I won't. But it's against my better judgment, Bradley.

BRADLEY. Thank you, Lucy.

LUCY. But if anything else happens to you, if he touches one hair on your head I'm calling the police.

BRADLEY. It won't happen again. Things are going to calm down. He won't be so stressed.

LUCY. Give me a hug, Bradley. *(Bradley hugs Lucy.)*

BRADLEY. Well, gotta get back to work. *(He puts on his sunglasses.)* You're on for brunch on Sunday at noon.

LUCY. Take care of yourself, Bradley.

BRADLEY. I will.

LUCY. Bradley?

BRADLEY. Yes.

LUCY. Did Mr. M mention anything about Mexico? Plane tickets? Hotel reservations?

BRADLEY. Not a thing.

LUCY. Oh.

BRADLEY. But sometimes he makes very important reservations himself.

LUCY. I'm sure he's already taken care of it. *(Emily enters. Doesn't see Bradley.)*

EMILY. Did Mr. Marmalade come for the tea party?

LUCY. No. It was his personal assistant. Bradley.

EMILY. He sent his assistant?

BRADLEY. This is your babysitter? How grim.

LUCY. Mr. Marmalade was too busy to come himself. He's under

14

a tremendous amount of pressure at work.

EMILY. What's Bradley like? Is he cute?

BRADLEY. I look awful! You should have seen me ten years ago.

LUCY. I'm worried about him. Bradley doesn't take care of himself.

BRADLEY. Maybe not like in the old days, but I try to stay fit.

EMILY. What do you mean he doesn't take care of himself? How can an imaginary personal assistant not take care of himself?

LUCY. He doesn't have much self-esteem. He gets pushed around.

BRADLEY. That's not fair, Lucy. That's only half the story.

EMILY. Sounds to me like he should get a new boss and you should get a new friend.

LUCY. Things are going to lighten up at work soon. And then Bradley won't have to sacrifice himself the way he does all the time.

BRADLEY. Thank you, Lucy. Goodbye. *(He disappears.)*

EMILY. When I was your age I liked to play line.

LUCY. How do you play line?

EMILY. You just get in a line and pretend to be waiting for something. I liked to wait for the bus.

LUCY. That doesn't sound very fun.

EMILY. Do you want to try it?

LUCY. I guess so.

EMILY. Here, you get behind me. *(They stand in a line.)* What are you waiting for?

LUCY. The butcher.

EMILY. No. We're at the bus station. What bus are you waiting for?

LUCY. The number seven.

EMILY. There is no bus number seven, Lucy.

LUCY. Then I guess it's going to be a long wait.

EMILY. I don't want to hurt your feelings, but you're not very good at Line. *(The doorbell rings.)*

LUCY. Who is that?

EMILY. It's George, my boyfriend.

LUCY. George isn't supposed to come over.

EMILY. He's already over.

LUCY. You two are going to have sex!

EMILY. We're going to do our math homework. *(She puts on lipstick and fusses with her hair.)* How do I look?

LUCY. Easy.

EMILY. Good. *(She tugs at her breasts, trying to make them look bigger. The doorbell rings again.)* Coming. I'm coming! *(Opens the door. George bounds in.)*

GEORGE. Hello, beautiful. *(George gives her a big kiss. Bends her backwards. Grabs her breasts.)*

EMILY. George!

GEORGE. Shut up, you love it.

EMILY. The kid.

GEORGE. Oh shit. Hiya, kid. Lucy, right? *(Lucy doesn't say anything.)* I got a surprise for you, Lucy. *(Calling.)* Larry!

EMILY. You brought Larry?

GEORGE. My folks are out playing bridge. I have to watch the stupid fucker. *(Calling.)* Larry! *(Sheepishly Larry enters. He's five years old.)* Larry, Lucy. Lucy, Larry. *(He picks up Emily and puts her over his shoulder.)* Have fun, kids. *(He carries her off, Emily shrieking in false protest.)*

LUCY. Shut the door. It's cold. *(Larry shuts the door gingerly.)* I'm Lucy.

LARRY. I'm Larry.

LUCY. Nice to meet you, Larry. *(She kisses him on the cheek.)*

LARRY. What are you doing?

LUCY. It's how people greet each other.

LARRY. In Europe maybe.

LUCY. In New York, too.

LARRY. Well I don't live either place. This is New Jersey.

LUCY. Fine. I'm sorry. I didn't mean to make you feel uncomfortable.

LARRY. You didn't make me feel uncomfortable. It was unfamiliar, that's all. There's a difference. *(Larry kisses her on the cheek.)*

LUCY. Hey! *(Larry walks around the room.)*

LARRY. This place is pretty nice.

LUCY. It's okay.

LARRY. So you live here with your parents and everything?

LUCY. It's just me and my mom. My dad, he divorced my mom when I was two, or something.

LARRY. My parents are divorced, too.

LUCY. Really?

LARRY. But my dad remarried. So I have a stepmom. And she had George from before so now I have a stepmom and a stepbrother. Do you have any brothers or sisters?

LUCY. No. It's just me.

LARRY. It's better that way. More time to yourself.

LUCY. You don't like George?

LARRY. George is an asshole.

LUCY. But there's somebody around. Somebody you can play with.

LARRY. We don't play. He beats me up all the time. It sucks.

LUCY. That's too bad.

LARRY. It's better to be by yourself. Trust me.

LUCY. You're probably right. But I get lonely sometimes.

LARRY. I don't get lonely.

LUCY. You don't?

LARRY. No. I hate being around people. I wish I could be by myself all the time.

LUCY. I'm alone all the time.

LARRY. We should trade lives. Like in that movie.

LUCY. Yeah.

LARRY. What makes you lonely?

LUCY. I don't know. Lots of things.

LARRY. Like what?

LUCY. Like I don't know. Like when I'm alone.

LARRY. You can be alone and not lonely.

LUCY. I can't.

LARRY. You should learn. You'd be a lot happier.

LUCY. Thanks for the tip.

LARRY. Where do you go to school?

LUCY. I haven't started school yet.

LARRY. I just got through with preschool.

LUCY. How was it?

LARRY. It was okay.

LUCY. I can't wait to start school.

LARRY. Yeah, it's pretty cool.

LUCY. Cool.

LARRY. I have to do it over.

LUCY. Why?

LARRY. They say I didn't have enough friends.

LUCY. You'll probably make more friends next year.

LARRY. I lied to you just then.

LUCY. Preschool's not cool?

LARRY. No, it is. When I said I didn't have any friends — that part was true — but that's not why they're making me repeat preschool.

LUCY. What's the real reason?

LARRY. Petty larceny.

LUCY. What's petty larceny?

LARRY. Small time thieving. That's what the cops call it. Petty larceny.

LUCY. What'd you steal?

LARRY. A bank shaped like a bunny. It had a slit on its head between the ears where we put money in so at the end of the year we could have a pizza party. But I stole the bunny bank and spent all the money.

LUCY. What happened to the pizza party?

LARRY. It was cancelled.

LUCY. What'd you spend the money on?

LARRY. Chocolate.

LUCY. I love chocolate!!!

LARRY. I ate so much I puked.

LUCY. I did that once, too.

LARRY. Anyway, that's the real reason I have to repeat preschool and I just wanted to tell you the truth. *(He takes off his jacket. We see bandages on his wrists.)*

LUCY. What are those?

LARRY. Bandages.

LUCY. What are they for?

LARRY. Cuts.

LUCY. How'd you get cuts on your wrists?

LARRY. That was the other reason I have to repeat preschool. I tried to commit suicide.

LUCY. Oh. I've never known anyone who tried to commit suicide.

LARRY. Well now you do.

LUCY. Cool.

LARRY. At the hospital they said I was the youngest suicide attempt in the history of New Jersey. The nurses took my picture and hung it in the lobby.

LUCY. Why'd you try to commit suicide?

LARRY. Everybody says, "Enjoy your childhood while it lasts," and I'm like, "I don't enjoy this at all." I'm not supposed to have a care in the world and all I can think about is how miserable life is. How much suffering there is in the world and how there doesn't seem to be any reason for it. I figured if this is the carefree part of my life then I don't want to see the part of my life that's supposed to be hard. So one morning before preschool I slit my wrists with George's razor blade. But my stepmom found me. It's too bad.

LUCY. Do you think you'll attempt suicide again?

LARRY. I don't know. I might. If I do, you can come to my funeral.

LUCY. I've never been to a funeral before.

LARRY. It's going to be the saddest thing in the history of America. Maybe even the world. I'm going to commit hara kari, like the samurai in Japan, but I'll still have an open casket and there will be good food like Cheetos and chocolate milk and everybody's going to cry and wonder how great my life could have been. Will you cry? At my funeral? If everybody else is.

LUCY. I'll try.

LARRY. That's all you can do. Try your best. That's what my step-mom says.

LUCY. Do you want to play Doctor with me?

LARRY. I don't know. How do you play?

LUCY. It's easy. You're the patient and I'm the doctor. I examine you to see what's the matter.

LARRY. But I feel fine.

LUCY. I know. It's just playing.

LARRY. Okay.

LUCY. Take your shirt off.

LARRY. No!

LUCY. How am I going to examine you with your shirt on?

LARRY. I don't know.

LUCY. Take it off.

LARRY. Fine. *(He takes it off.)*

LUCY. What seems to be the problem?

LARRY. Nothing. I feel fine.

LUCY. I'll try again, okay? What seems to be the problem?

LARRY. My wrists are kind of sore.

LUCY. No, not what's really the matter. Pretend.

LARRY. Oh. I'm having chest pains.

LUCY. That's very serious. Let me listen to your heart.

LARRY. Okay. *(Lucy listens to Larry's chest.)*

LUCY. You might need a heart transplant.

LARRY. A heart transplant!

LUCY. Do you have health insurance?

LARRY. Not that I know of.

LUCY. I'm afraid there's nothing I can do.

LARRY. But I'll die.

LUCY. I'm afraid so.

LARRY. That stinks.

LUCY. Health care in this country. What are you gonna do?

LARRY. Wait a sec. I do have health insurance. *(He whips out an imaginary card.)*

LUCY. Wonderful! Let's get you that new heart. *(They do a quick heart transplant.)* How's that new heart?

LARRY. I don't have the chest pains anymore.

LUCY. You've made a complete recovery. Could you please slip off your pants.

LARRY. What?

LUCY. I have to check something out. It's a post-surgery thing.

LARRY. You gave me a heart transplant, Lucy, I don't see what my pants have to do with it.

LUCY. Call me Doctor, please. This is how you play, Larry. I'm the doctor and you're the patient. Take your pants off.

LARRY. Okay, okay. *(He takes down his pants. He's wearing little boy underwear, preferably red.)*

LUCY. Cough. *(Larry coughs. She puts her hand down his pants.)* Cough. *(Larry coughs.)*

LARRY. Are you sure this is how you play Doctor?

LUCY. I'm sure.

LARRY. When I was in the hospital it wasn't like this.

LUCY. This is a private practice. *(She takes her hand out of his pants.)* I am finished with my examination. You seem to be in very good shape. I hope the heart transplant helps you live a long life.

LARRY. Thank you, Doctor.

LUCY. Now we switch. Now you're the doctor and I'm the patient. *(She lies down.)*

LARRY. Okay.

LUCY. Doctor, I'm in pain.

LARRY. Where does it hurt?

LUCY. Everywhere. You're going to have to examine me from head to toe. *(Larry begins to examine her.)*

III.

CONCERNING COUNTLESS MORE HARDSHIPS WHICH LUCY ENDURED WITH REGARD TO HER IMAGINARY FRIENDS, IF YOU CAN EVEN CALL THEM THAT

Lucy and Larry are on the couch, lying down, wrapped up in a blanket. Lucy watches Larry sleep. She brushes his hair with her hand. Bradley appears. He's on crutches. His arm is in a sling. He has two black eyes. His nose is bleeding. He's in really bad shape.

LUCY. Bradley!

BRADLEY. Oh, Lucy.

LUCY. It's not what it looks like.

BRADLEY. How could you?

LUCY. It just happened. We were playing Doctor —

BRADLEY. — You played Doctor with him?

LUCY. I was lonely. And he's the sweetest boy. He tried to commit suicide because he said there was no reason for all the suffering in the world.

BRADLEY. Mr. Marmalade is not going to be pleased.

LUCY. He doesn't have to know.

BRADLEY. He has a right to know. Do you know why he sent me here?

LUCY. No. *(Bradley opens his briefcase. Takes out a box of chocolates shaped like a heart.)*

BRADLEY. He wanted me to bring you these.

LUCY. Chocolates!

BRADLEY. Read the card.

LUCY. I can't read yet.

BRADLEY. I'll read it. *(Reading.)* Dearest Lucy, My heart breaks every second I'm away from you. All my love, Mr. M *(Not reading.)* And this is how you repay him! *(Bradley rips up the note.)*

LUCY. You don't have to tell Mr. M., Bradley. I didn't tell anyone that he hit you.

BRADLEY. That was an accident.

LUCY. So was this. Please, Bradley. Pleeeeeeeaaase.

BRADLEY. Fine. I won't tell him.

LUCY. Thank you, Bradley.

BRADLEY. But don't let it happen again.

LUCY. It won't.

BRADLEY. Because Mr. Marmalade cares so much about you. And my favorite part of this job is coming to see you. I would hate for that to change.

LUCY. I know. You're right. I don't know what I was thinking.

BRADLEY. Good. I feel better. We all make mistakes. Everyone deserves a second chance.

LUCY. Thank you, Bradley.

BRADLEY. Mr. Marmalade was also wondering if he could change brunch on Sunday to two o'clock.

LUCY. Two o'clock is fine.

BRADLEY. Good. I'll pencil you in. *(He pencils her in.)* Well, I'd better be off. *(He begins to wobble off.)*

LUCY. What happened to you, Bradley?

BRADLEY. Skiing accident.

LUCY. You don't look so good.

BRADLEY. You should see the tree I hit.

LUCY. Are you sure everything's okay?

BRADLEY. Of course.

LUCY. You would tell me if it wasn't, right?

BRADLEY. Of course I would, Lucy.

LUCY. Take care of yourself, Bradley.

BRADLEY. You too, Lucy. *(He disappears. She waits for Larry to wake up. He doesn't. She coughs. Nothing. She drops something on the floor with a loud bang. Larry wakes up suddenly.)*

LARRY. Hello.

LUCY. Hello.

LARRY. Did you sleep?

LUCY. No.

LARRY. I slept like a baby.

LUCY. You have to go.

LARRY. What?

LUCY. You have to leave now.

LARRY. Why?

LUCY. Because I said so.

LARRY. That's not a reason.

LUCY. Yes it is.

LARRY. Did I do something wrong?

LUCY. No. I can't explain. I'm sorry. You just have to leave.

LARRY. Right now?

LUCY. Right now.

LARRY. Okay. *(He gets up. Puts on his clothes.)* Can I see you again?

LUCY. No.

LARRY. Do you have a boyfriend or something?

LUCY. Sort of.

LARRY. Oh.

LUCY. What?

LARRY. I just wanted to be your boyfriend, that's all.

LUCY. Well, you can't be my boyfriend.

LARRY. Okay. No. I understand. It's just —

LUCY. What?

LARRY. Nothing.

LUCY. What is it?

LARRY. It's just … I don't know. I've never been as happy as I am right now.

LUCY. Really?

LARRY. Yeah. I'm sorry, I'll go.

LUCY. No. You can stay another minute. What were you saying?

LARRY. I mean, I don't know if I've ever even been happy before right now. You know how earlier I was saying I don't ever get lonely? I was lying.

LUCY. You lie a lot.

LARRY. I'm lonely all the time. Like always. Like for my whole life. That's why I tried to kill myself. But now, I'm not lonely. I'm happy.

LUCY. I'm happy with you too, Larry.

LARRY. Then what's the problem? *(Bradley appears on his crutches. It's important he's not in Larry's line of vision, because Larry could see him.)*

LUCY. It's complicated.

LARRY. No, it's simple.

LUCY. Larry, you don't understand what you're talking about. You have to go right now, okay?

LARRY. You don't want me to be your boyfriend?

LUCY. No, I'm sorry.

LARRY. I understand. No, I don't understand. But I'll go anyway.

LUCY. I shouldn't have played Doctor with you. I shouldn't have

23

led you on.

LARRY. Yeah. Okay. Maybe I'll see you at school.

LUCY. Yeah. See you at school. *(He's gone.)* Are you happy?

BRADLEY. Don't be angry with me, Lucy. I'm just doing my job.

LUCY. I'm not talking to you right now, Bradley.

BRADLEY. Let's talk about it over a cup of tea. Do you have any tea?

LUCY. I'm fresh out.

BRADLEY. Maybe I have some. *(He begins to open his briefcase but Lucy slams it shut.)*

LUCY. You should leave, Bradley.

BRADLEY. We have to get our stories straight, Lucy. Mr. Marmalade is going to wonder where I've been and if our stories don't match up I promise you I'll be in as much trouble as you are. Probably more.

LUCY. Tell him the truth.

BRADLEY. Don't be ridiculous. I'll tell him you weren't feeling well and that I made you some chicken soup. *(George comes down the stairs, triumphant. Emily follows him.)*

GEORGE. Come here, I need a babysitter. *(He pinches her. She giggles.)*

BRADLEY. Okay, Lucy? Please.

EMILY. Not in front of Lucy.

GEORGE. Hiya, Lucy.

LUCY. Hello.

BRADLEY. You weren't feeling well. I made you chicken soup.

LUCY. *(To Bradley.)* Fine.

GEORGE. Did you and Larry get along?

LUCY. Yes. He's a very sweet boy.

GEORGE. Where is the little shitbird?

LUCY. He left.

GEORGE. What do you mean he left?

LUCY. I asked him to leave and he left. Unlike some people.

BRADLEY. Mum's the word. Goodbye, Lucy. *(Bradley disappears.)*

GEORGE. You're fucking kidding me.

LUCY. No.

GEORGE. My parents are gonna fucking kill me. He's suicidal, you know.

LUCY. He was suicidal. He's not anymore.

EMILY. I'm sure he's fine, George.

GEORGE. Fuck do you know about it? If there's anything wrong with him I'm gonna sue your ass, you little bitch. *(He goes.)*

EMILY. Asshole.

LUCY. How was your date upstairs?

EMILY. It was fine.

LUCY. Did you two do it?

EMILY. I'm not going to discuss it with you, Lucy.

LUCY. I hope you used protection.

EMILY. Listen, it's like 10:30 and I've got school in the morning. I kind of have to go. (Mr. Marmalade appears. He smokes a cigarette. A Newport.)

LUCY. You couldn't stay for like another half an hour?

EMILY. I'm sorry, Lucy. I can't. Tell your mom she can pay me next time.

LUCY. Okay. (She goes.)

MR. MARMALADE. Good evening.

LUCY. I thought we were having brunch on Sunday.

MR. MARMALADE. Some time freed up tonight. Thought I'd drop by if that's okay.

LUCY. It's fine with me.

MR. MARMALADE. You're not happy to see me?

LUCY. No, I am. It's a surprise, that's all.

MR. MARMALADE. Bradley said you weren't feeling well. He said he made you some chicken soup.

LUCY. (A little cough.) That's right. He did.

MR. MARMALADE. You mind if I sit?

LUCY. Be my guest.

MR. MARMALADE. Thanks. (He falls into the couch with a thud.) My feet are killing me. (Takes off his shoes.)

LUCY. How was work?

MR. MARMALADE. Fucking nightmare. You have no idea.

LUCY. Have you been drinking?

MR. MARMALADE. I had a few after work to unwind. You would too if you'd ever worked a day in your life.

LUCY. I wouldn't know.

MR. MARMALADE. No, you wouldn't.

LUCY. Have you made the reservations?

MR. MARMALADE. Reservations for what?

LUCY. Mexico. Cabo San Lucas. First class across the board.

MR. MARMALADE. No, I haven't made the reservations yet.

LUCY. Are you going to have Bradley do it?

MR. MARMALADE. Get off my ass, all right? Jesus. I just got here. I just fucking sat down and you just start nagging me about Mexico.

LUCY. We're still going to go, right?

25

MR. MARMALADE. Sure we are. I'll do it tomorrow, okay? *(Mr. Marmalade opens his briefcase. Takes out a vial of cocaine. He cuts two big lines. Rolls up a twenty-dollar bill.)*

LUCY. Mr. Marmalade, is that cocaine?

MR. MARMALADE. What? I'm sorry. You want some?

LUCY. No. I don't want any cocaine.

MR. MARMALADE. Suit yourself. *(He blows a line.)* You sure? This is some good shit.

LUCY. I'm sure. *(He blows the second line.)*

MR. MARMALADE. Hey, let's play House. "Hey honey, I'm home!"

LUCY. No.

MR. MARMALADE. That's when you say, "How was work?"

LUCY. I don't want to play House with you.

MR. MARMALADE. And I say, "It sucked balls. But somebody's gotta fucking provide for this fucking family, you lazy bitch." *(Silence.)* You don't want to play House with me?

LUCY. Not like this.

MR. MARMALADE. What do you mean not like this?

LUCY. When you're drunk and high.

MR. MARMALADE. What? Who's high? This is like a cup of coffee. I don't even feel it. Hey, Lucy, I work twenty hours a day you know? I gotta stay alert.

LUCY. I'm still not playing.

MR. MARMALADE. Fuck that. I want to play House.

LUCY. I won't play House with you.

MR. MARMALADE. Then let's play Doctor. Come here. My prostate hurts. I might need surgery.

LUCY. I'm not going to play Doctor with you.

MR. MARMALADE. My prostate hurts.

LUCY. Get out!

MR. MARMALADE. Fine. I don't need this shit anyway. *(He struggles to stand up. He opens his briefcase the wrong way. Everything falls out. Filthy porno magazines, dildos, whips, drugs, maybe an inflatable blow-up doll with the mouth open for blowjobs.)* Oh shit. *(He gets on his hands and begins to pick up the magazines and dildos.)* These aren't even mine. I was just holding onto them for a friend.

LUCY. Get out.

MR. MARMALADE. Okay, okay. Jesus Christ. So sorry to disturb. I'll see you at brunch on Sunday.

LUCY. No you won't.

MR. MARMALADE. What?

LUCY. I don't want to see you anymore.

MR. MARMALADE. Fuck you talking about?

LUCY. I don't want to play House with you anymore. Or Doctor. I don't want to go to Mexico with you. I don't want to play with you at all.

MR. MARMALADE. These pornos aren't even mine, I swear.

LUCY. I don't care about the pornos.

MR. MARMALADE. Because of a little coke?

LUCY. Because you're a bad person. Because you neglect me. Because you beat up Bradley. Because I deserve a lot better than you.

MR. MARMALADE. Is there somebody else?

LUCY. What do you mean?

MR. MARMALADE. I mean is there a replacement of me? Somebody who plays House and Doctor with you.

LUCY. No.

MR. MARMALADE. You're fucking lying to me. There's somebody else.

LUCY. There might be somebody else.

MR. MARMALADE. What's his name?

LUCY. He's nobody you know.

MR. MARMALADE. What's his fucking name?

LUCY. Larry.

MR. MARMALADE. What the fuck kind of name is Larry?

LUCY. I don't know. It's his name.

MR. MARMALADE. Fuck! I can't believe this shit. What's this clown do?

LUCY. Do?

MR. MARMALADE. Do? Do? Do? Do do do do do. What's his fucking job? What does fucking Larry fucking do?

LUCY. He doesn't do anything.

MR. MARMALADE. He's unemployed.

LUCY. He's five.

MR. MARMALADE. Fuck does that mean he's five?

LUCY. He's five years old.

MR. MARMALADE. Let's not go crazy here, Lucy. You're not going to leave me for a toddler. In business there's always a compromise.

LUCY. There's no compromise.

MR. MARMALADE. I'll cut back at work.

LUCY. I'm sorry. No.

MR. MARMALADE. I'll get help for the drugs. Okay? Lucy? I'm totally willing to admit I have a drug problem. Okay? Twelve-step programs. Rehab. Just don't leave me.

LUCY. I'm sorry, Mr. Marmalade.

MR. MARMALADE. You fucking cunt.

LUCY. You're high. You don't mean what you're saying.

MR. MARMALADE. News flash! I've been high since the beginning, okay?

LUCY. I never meant to hurt you. *(He hits her in the face. She falls to the ground. Her lip bleeds.)*

MR. MARMALADE. You never meant to hurt me? *(He spits on her. Larry appears.)* Who the fuck is this? *(She won't tell.)* Answer me, bitch. Who the fuck is this?

LARRY. I'm Larry.

LUCY. Larry?

LARRY. I'll handle this, Lucy.

MR. MARMALADE. You're Larry. This is fucking Larry!!!

LARRY. Shut up, dude.

MR. MARMALADE. Fuck you, Larry. This is private.

LARRY. You're leaving.

MR. MARMALADE. I'm not leaving.

LARRY. Yes you are.

MR. MARMALADE. Who's gonna make me?

LARRY. I am.

MR. MARMALADE. You and what army?

LARRY. Just me.

MR. MARMALADE. Fuck you, Larry. *(Mr. Marmalade takes a swing at Larry, but Larry dodges it, and quickly puts Mr. Marmalade into a very painful submission hold.)*

LARRY. I'm a green belt in Brazilian Jujitsu.

MR. MARMALADE. Easy, Larry.

LARRY. I can break your arm in five places.

MR. MARMALADE. Let's not do anything we're gonna regret, Larry.

LARRY. You think I'd regret kicking your ass?

MR. MARMALADE. There will be legal ramifications. That's all I'm saying, okay?

LARRY. You're leaving.

MR. MARMALADE. Owwwww. Fine. I'm leaving.

LARRY. And you're not allowed to come back. Do we understand each other, dude?

MR. MARMALADE. Loud and clear, Larry. Just let go of my arm.

LARRY. You're not going to bother Lucy anymore. Right?

MR. MARMALADE. Owwww. Right. Right. *(Larry lets go. Mr. Marmalade gathers all of his magazines and dildos and puts them in his briefcase.)* You better hope there's no nerve damage, you little shit. Expect to hear from my attorney in due course. *(He disappears.)*

LARRY. Are you okay? Are you bleeding?

LUCY. Maybe a little bit.

LARRY. Here, let me. *(He dabs at the blood with a bandage from his wrist.)* Who was that guy?

LUCY. He used to be my friend. His name's Mr. Marmalade.

LARRY. That guy was your friend?

LUCY. People change. He used to be a good guy.

LARRY. Well, he's not anymore.

LUCY. Larry?

LARRY. Yes, Lucy?

LUCY. Do you know how to play House?

IV.

OF WHAT HAPPENED BETWEEN LUCY AND LARRY: ONE OF THE MOST IMPORTANT SCENES IN THIS WHOLE PLAY P.S. IT'S LATER THAT SAME NIGHT, EVEN THOUGH IT SEEMS IMPOSSIBLE THAT YOUNG PEOPLE WOULD BE UP AT SUCH HOURS

Larry enters. He's wearing his dad's suit. It's much too big for him. He carries a child's record player with a handle.

LARRY. Honey, I'm home!

LUCY. *(Offstage.)* I'm in the kitchen, honey! Just a second. *(He turns on the record player. Greasy French romance music plays. I suggest Yves Montand. He opens his suit and takes out a big bag of potato chips, preferably Cool Ranch Doritos. He reaches into his sleeve and takes out one of those really long licorice ropes. Then another. Maybe another. In his pants are Gummi Bears, Popsicles, candy bars, sticks of gum, Twinkies, Ho-Hos, pork rinds, Funions, Oreos, Nutter Butters, some EZ Cheese and Redi Whip whipped cream. It is a cornucopia of junk food. He is very proud of his dinner. Wait. The last touch is a single rose which he had somewhere in his pants. He cradles it tenderly and puts it in a vase. Lucy enters. She wears the dress her mother didn't pick and most of her makeup. Lucy walks in high heels which she doesn't know how to do.)*

LARRY. Close your eyes, close your eyes. *(Lucy closes her eyes. Larry guides her to the table.)* Okay, open 'em.

LUCY. Oh my God!

LARRY. Dinner is served.

LUCY. Larry! It's beautiful.

LARRY. Let's just say 7-11 was kind to us.

LUCY. It looks wonderful. Thank you so much. What should we eat first?

LARRY. First, a toast. *(He pulls out some chocolate milk.)*

LUCY. Chocolate milk!

LARRY. Our favorite! *(He presents it to her like it was champagne, over his arm. He lets her smell the cap. She nods in approval. Larry pours two full glasses.)*

LUCY. What are we toasting to?

LARRY. To happiness.

LUCY. To happiness. *(They clink glasses and drink.)* Mmmmm. Good, huh?

LARRY. Delicious.

LUCY. Let's eat. I'm famished. *(Larry sits but Lucy waits by her chair.)*

LARRY. Why don't you sit down? *(Lucy just stares at her chair.)* Sorry, dear. *(Larry runs over to her chair and pulls it out for her.)*

LUCY. Thank you, dear.

LARRY. My pleasure, dear. *(Larry unfolds her paper towel napkin and puts it in Lucy's lap.)* Bon appetit! *(Larry returns to his seat and they both busily unwrap different snacks and treats. They eat for a bit.)*

LUCY. Could you pass the Doritos?

LARRY. Of course. *(He passes the Doritos.)*

LUCY. Thank you, dear.

LARRY. My pleasure, dear. *(Larry pours some EZ cheese into his mouth. Not be outdone, Lucy pours some whipped cream into her mouth.)*

LUCY. I have some very big news, dear.

LARRY. I'm all ears.

LUCY. Are you ready?

LARRY. I think so.

LUCY. I'm pregnant.

LARRY. Really?

LUCY. I got the test results from the doctor this afternoon.

LARRY. Are you serious?

LUCY. You're not happy!

LARRY. No, Lucy, are you for real pregnant or are you play pregnant?

LUCY. Play pregnant.

LARRY. Oh! Wonderful news! I'm so happy! I'm going to be a father. It's mine, isn't it?

LUCY. Of course it's yours.

LARRY. That's good.

LUCY. You don't sound like you're really happy.

LARRY. Of course I'm happy.

LUCY. I know it's a bit of a shock.

LARRY. It did come as a surprise.

LUCY. But a wonderful surprise I hope. What are you thinking about?

LARRY. I don't know if a baby is what we need right now, you know? I don't know if I'm ready to be a father. You know, and I don't know if I really want to bring a child into this world in general, let alone now with you. I'm not very happy that I was born and don't really feel like I'm in the position to make anyone else go through this.

LUCY. You're entitled to your opinion. But I'm going to have it one way or another.

LARRY. Fine, you know. That's your choice. I totally respect your right to choose.

LUCY. Good.

LARRY. Good. Could you pass the Oreos?

LUCY. Here. *(Gives Larry the Oreos.)*

LARRY. Lucy?

LUCY. Yes, what is it?

LARRY. Will you feel my head? I think I might have a fever. *(She feels his head.)*

LUCY. You're fine.

LARRY. I think it might be my uterus.

LUCY. You don't have a uterus.

LARRY. Fine, I don't have a uterus. It's just that we don't play Doctor anymore.

LUCY. Now we're playing House.

LARRY. So when you play House you can't play Doctor?

LUCY. That's right. They are two very different games.

LARRY. That's stupid.

LUCY. Larry!

LARRY. What? That's ridiculous.

LUCY. Can we just enjoy our dinner that you worked so hard to provide?

LARRY. I stole all this food, Lucy.

LUCY. I don't know what you're talking about.

LARRY. You know I did.

LUCY. I really don't.

LARRY. I'm not playing House anymore. *(Larry turns off the music.)*

LUCY. We were having such a wonderful time. We're pregnant with our first child. What's the matter?

LARRY. Nothing. *(He eats.)*

LUCY. I wish you'd say something. Tell me about work.

LARRY. It was fine.

LUCY. It wasn't too busy?

LARRY. It was fine. *(A cactus and a sunflower appear. They can talk.)*

CACTUS. Hello.

SUNFLOWER. Can we come in?

CACTUS. It's cold.

LARRY. Sure. Come on in. Are you hungry?

CACTUS. I'm famished.

SUNFLOWER. Me too.

LUCY. Larry? What are those?

LARRY. Those are my imaginary friends.

LUCY. I thought it was going to be just you and me. We're playing House.

LARRY. They can play House, too. It's good to see you. How are you guys doing?

CACTUS. I'm hungry.

SUNFLOWER. I'm cold.

CACTUS. I'm hungry and cold.

SUNFLOWER. Me too.

CACTUS. Who's the skirt?

LARRY. That's Lucy. We're playing House.

CACTUS. She's hot.

SUNFLOWER. Good work, Larry.

LUCY. I can hear what you're saying.

CACTUS. Oh. Excuse me.

SUNFLOWER. Nice to meet you, Lucy. You have a beautiful home.

CACTUS. It looks like a great spread.

LUCY. I suppose there's enough food. Even for uninvited guests.

LARRY. I didn't know they were coming.

LUCY. Can I offer you plants some chocolate milk?

CACTUS. Yes, please. I'm very thirsty.

SUNFLOWER. I love chocolate milk. *(She pours them glasses of chocolate milk.)*

LUCY. What should we toast to?

CACTUS. To the happy couple.

SUNFLOWER. To the happy couple. *(They all drink.)*

LUCY. And what exactly do you plants do? *(The plants eat very messily.)*

SUNFLOWER. I just sit by the window and look at the sun.

CACTUS. Me too.

SUNFLOWER. Sometimes I think about water.

CACTUS. I think about water all the time.

LARRY. We're playing House.

CACTUS. I've never played House.

LARRY. It's easy.

SUNFLOWER. We usually play Cowboys and Indians. I'm always the Indian.

LARRY. Just make something up.

CACTUS. Like what?

LARRY. Like a job.

CACTUS. Oh. Okay. I'm a stuntman.

SUNFLOWER. I make submarines.

LUCY. That's very interesting. Larry is a banker. He makes a very good salary and great benefits.

LARRY. Lucy!

LUCY. What? It's true, isn't it? We're among friends. They can know how successful you are, can't they?

LARRY. I guess so.

LUCY. What have you plants been reading?

CACTUS. I don't know how to read.

SUNFLOWER. I can read my name.

LUCY. Larry just finished *The Sound and The Fury*. It's a very difficult book by William Faulkner. *(One of the plants throws a piece of food.)* Do you know who William Faulkner is?

CACTUS. Don't throw that at me, dick.

SUNFLOWER. You're the dick.

CACTUS. You're dick*less*. *(They throw food at each other.)*

LUCY. Larry, stop them.

LARRY. Hey guys, take it easy.

CACTUS and SUNFLOWER. Dick! *(They throw food at Larry. Larry throws food back.)*

LARRY. You're the dicks! *(It quickly turns into a full fledged food fight. It's really messy. The vase with the flower get knocked to the ground and breaks. Everybody stops.)*

LUCY. Get out.

CACTUS. I'm sorry.

SUNFLOWER. It was his fault.

LUCY. Get the fuck out of my house. *(The plants start crying.)*

CACTUS. We're really sorry.

SUNFLOWER. We'll be good.

CACTUS. Can we stay?

LUCY. No. I want you out of this house.

LARRY. Sorry, guys. You heard the old ball and chain.

LUCY. You too, Larry.

LARRY. What?

LUCY. Get out.

LARRY. But …

LUCY. I don't want to play House with you anymore.

LARRY. But …

LUCY. No buts.

LARRY. Our marriage.

LUCY. It's annulled.

LARRY. What about the baby? Shouldn't we stay together for the sake of the baby?

LUCY. It's not even yours.

SUNFLOWER. Cuckolded.

CACTUS. That's some cold shit.

LARRY. I'll see you plants later.

SUNFLOWER. Good night.

CACTUS. Don't let the bedbugs bite.

SUNFLOWER. I hate bedbugs.

CACTUS. Me too.

SUNFLOWER. Me three.

CACTUS. Me four.

SUNFLOWER. What's after four?

CACTUS. I don't know.

SUNFLOWER. Me neither. *(They're gone.)*

LARRY. OK, they're gone. We can keep playing.

LUCY. No, Larry.

LARRY. I'm sorry, all right? Those plants are dicks. I shouldn't have invited them over to play House with us.

LUCY. You should go, too.

LARRY. We can play something else. We can play Cowboys and Indians.

LUCY. No.

LARRY. Cops and Robbers.

LUCY. No.

LARRY. Fine. We don't have to play anything at all. We can just sit here. We don't even have to talk.

LUCY. I don't want you here anymore, Larry.

LARRY. We were happy! We weren't lonely anymore.

LUCY. I was here with you, Larry, but I was still lonely.

LARRY. Oh. Okay. I'll go. Goodbye, Lucy.

LUCY. Goodbye, Larry. *(He goes, with his tail between his legs. Lucy looks at the disgusting room. Sighs and begins to clean up a little. Mr. Marmalade appears with a trash bag and rubber gloves. He's dressed immaculately in his suit.)*

MR. MARMALADE. Good evening.

LUCY. What are you doing here?

MR. MARMALADE. Looks like you could use an extra pair of hands.

LUCY. That would be nice.

MR. MARMALADE. Allow me. *(He picks up the rose from the floor and gives it to her while on one knee.)* A rose for milady.

LUCY. Thank you, fair sir. *(She curtsies. He cleans up all the junk food.)* You don't have to clean up, Mr. Marmalade.

MR. MARMALADE. It's my pleasure. Who made this mess?

LUCY. Larry and his plant friends.

MR. MARMALADE. How is Larry?

LUCY. We broke up.

MR. MARMALADE. I'm sorry to hear that.

LUCY. Yeah, right.

MR. MARMALADE. No, really. It took some getting used to, but I think you were good together. Probably better than you and I were. He seemed like a good guy.

LUCY. He wasn't. *(Mr. Marmalade takes goggles out of his briefcase. Hands them to Lucy.)*

MR. MARMALADE. Put these goggles on.

LUCY. I love goggles. *(He puts his own goggles on. She puts goggles on. Mr. Marmalade whips out a large leaf blower.)* What's that, Mr. Marmalade?

MR. MARMALADE. It's my SuckBlow 6000.

LUCY. It's really big. *(He turns it on and blows all of the junk food off the stage. It's really loud and you shouldn't really be able to hear what he's talking about.)*

MR. MARMALADE. I won it in a poker game.

LUCY. What?

MR. MARMALADE. I bluffed. I only had a pair of twos but I just kept raising and raising until finally my friend Ramon put up this SuckBlow. Ramon was never much of a card player. But I think he was sort of happy to get rid of it because his ex-girlfriend Rita gave it to him so every time he blew leaves he thought of her.* *(He's fin-*

36

ished. He turns it off. [If Mr. Marmalade needs more time to get the stage clean here is some more for him to say: "Rita was a real character. She had a tattoo on her upper inner thigh that says 'Slippery When Wet.' You're probably wondering how I know that. One night we got wasted doing tequila shooters and she pulled down her pants in the middle of the bar, and I'm like whoa, Rita, you're my friend's girlfriend, I don't want to see your upper inner thigh. But there she was in the middle of the bar with her pants down. Anyway that's how I saw the tattoo. Their breakup was a real mess, Rita and Ramon's. She burned most of his stuff, even his antique toy collection which he loved more than anything. Like I said, Rita was a real character."])

LUCY. What?

MR. MARMALADE. Don't worry about it. *(He puts the SuckBlow away.)* Where were we?

LUCY. We were talking about Larry.

MR. MARMALADE. I could talk to him if you want.

LUCY. Let's talk about you. How's work?

MR. MARMALADE. I quit.

LUCY. You quit?

MR. MARMALADE. I realized I'm not getting any younger. What am I doing busting my hump twenty hours a day? Carpe diem, you know?

LUCY. You look great.

MR. MARMALADE. I went through rehab.

LUCY. Really?

MR. MARMALADE. I did detox in Newark. Then I was in a halfway house up in New Haven for awhile.

LUCY. That's wonderful, Mr. Marmalade. I'm so proud of you.

MR. MARMALADE. My sponsor's an ex-junkie. He was blind. When he was using he ran out of veins so he shot up in his eyes. He changed my life. I'm sorry, you don't want to hear about all this stuff.

LUCY. No, it's fascinating. I can't believe you've changed so much.

MR. MARMALADE. I did it for you, Lucy.

LUCY. Really?

MR. MARMALADE. Of course. It's always been for you. I made you a pair of moccasins.

LUCY. No you didn't. *(He whips out a pair of handmade moccasins.)*

MR. MARMALADE. What are you, a size three?

LUCY. Three and a half.

MR. MARMALADE. You've grown. See if they fit. *(He puts the moccasins on her feet.)* We did all sorts of craftwork at the halfway house. Basket weaving. Pottery painting. Needlepoint. I even learned bird calling. I can call a bluebird from fifty yards away. *(He does a little bird call.)*

LUCY. It sounds wonderful.

MR. MARMALADE. Take a walk around.

LUCY. They're nice. Comfortable. *(She walks.)*

MR. MARMALADE. I'm sorry.

LUCY. No, they fit fine.

MR. MARMALADE. No. For before. I fucked up. Excuse me. I screwed up. I was out of control. That's step nine. Apologize to everyone I hurt when I was using.

LUCY. It seems like you've really turned over a new leaf.

MR. MARMALADE. Are you willing to give me a second chance?

LUCY. Yes.

MR. MARMALADE. Thank you, Lucy. *(He picks her up and hugs her.)* Are you hungry?

LUCY. Starving. Those plants ruined my dinner.

MR. MARMALADE. Bradley! *(He snaps his fingers and Bradley appears with a big boat of sushi. He looks great. No injuries at all.)*

BRADLEY. Good evening, Lucy.

LUCY. Good evening, Bradley. *(Lucy looks at the sushi boat.)*

MR. MARMALADE. Fresh from Nobu. Monkfish Pate with Caviar, Sashimi Salad, Sea Urchin Tempura, Whitefish with Ponzu, Bradley's favorite, Fresh Yellowtail with Jalapeno.

BRADLEY. I love jalapeno!

LUCY. It looks delicious.

MR. MARMALADE. It's all for you, Lucy.

LUCY. Thank you, Mr. Marmalade. *(He snaps his fingers. Three men in white tuxedos enter with lots of roses, candelabras, champagne, fancy desserts. It's a whirlwind.)*

MR. MARMALADE. Roses fresh from the Garden of Versailles. Candles handcrafted from white whale blubber. Ice cream from the milk of cows who eat only chocolate.

LUCY. This is all for me?

MR. MARMALADE. It's all for you, Lucy.

LUCY. I don't know what to say.

MR. MARMALADE. Eat. Drink. Enjoy. *(She eats.)* Bradley, if you please. *(Bradley leads the waiters. Maybe instruments are played, if the actors know how. A violin. A guitar. A clarinet. They sing a sweet, slow love song all the way through. It should be the French song from before.*

Bradley sings in French very sweetly. Lucy eats for awhile.) Lucy, would you do me the honor?

LUCY. It would be my pleasure. *(Mr. Marmalade and Lucy dance sweetly, slowly, beautifully. They look into each other's eyes. She buries her head in his shoulder. She dances on top of his shoes. After the dance is finished, Lucy curtsies and Mr. Marmalade bows. They applaud the band.)* Thank you, Mr. Marmalade.

MR. MARMALADE. My pleasure. This is the happiest night of my life.

LUCY. Mine too.

MR. MARMALADE. I almost forgot. Look what I've got. *(He whips out some plane tickets.)* Mexico! Cabo. You and me. We leave tonight. First class across the board!

LUCY. Mr. Marmalade!

MR. MARMALADE. Bradley, go get Lucy's suitcase. *(Bradley goes upstairs.)* That will be all for tonight, gentlemen. Thank you very much. *(They disappear with all of the stuff they brought on.)* I missed you, Lucy.

LUCY. You did?

MR. MARMALADE. Terribly. I thought of you all the time. It didn't matter what I was doing or who I was with. Whether I was basketweaving or talking to my sponsor about OD'ing on bad horse. Did you think of me?

LUCY. Yes. Always. *(He kisses her on the mouth.)* Mr. Marmalade!

MR. MARMALADE. Is that okay? I'm sorry. I shouldn't have.

LUCY. No. It's okay.

MR. MARMALADE. Are you sure it's okay?

LUCY. Yes. I'm sure.

MR. MARMALADE. Because I've wanted to. Before. For a long time.

LUCY. I know. Me too.

MR. MARMALADE. Really?

LUCY. You couldn't tell?

MR. MARMALADE. No. I don't know. I thought maybe. I didn't want to get my hopes up, you know?

LUCY. I know.

MR. MARMALADE. I feel like I'm going to die when I say goodbye to you.

LUCY. Me too.

MR. MARMALADE. I don't want to leave ever again.

LUCY. I don't want you to.

MR. MARMALADE. When we get back from Mexico is it all right if I stay here with you?

LUCY. Of course. I've always wanted you to stay.

MR. MARMALADE. You have?

LUCY. I've never wanted anything else.

MR. MARMALADE. This is going to be great.

LUCY. Do you want to have children?

MR. MARMALADE. I want it all. A home of our own. A white picket fence. Lots of kids running around.

LUCY. Me too. That's exactly what I want.

MR. MARMALADE. Everything we were promised is in our reach, Lucy. We can be so happy. *(Bradley comes back with the suitcase.)*

BRADLEY. All packed.

MR. MARMALADE. Are you ready to go?

LUCY. Yes.

MR. MARMALADE. Let's go.

BRADLEY. *Vaminos! (They go.)*

V.

OF WHAT HAPPENED TO LUCY AND
MR. MARMALADE — A SAD AND HORRIBLE SCENE
IN THIS PLAY WHICH MAY BE VERY DIFFICULT
TO WATCH FOR THE SQUEAMISH

A baby cries in the kitchen. Mr. Marmalade watches television. He wears a wifebeater. No shoes or socks. He drinks a cheap domestic beer and smokes Newports. The place is filthy. Worse than before. Beer cans. Old food. Pizza boxes. At least a year's worth of shit and grime.

MR. MARMALADE. Will you shut that kid up?

LUCY. *(Offstage.)* What?

MR. MARMALADE. Shut the kid up! I'm trying to watch TV.

LUCY. *(Offstage.)* I can't hear you, honey. The baby's crying.

MR. MARMALADE. Jesus Christ. I know the baby's crying. I can hear the baby crying. I want you to stop the baby from crying.

LUCY. *(Offstage.)* Just a second! *(She comes dressed in her mother's slip, carrying a baby wrapped in a blanket.)*

MR. MARMALADE. Leave the kid in the kitchen.

LUCY. Just tell me what you want.

MR. MARMALADE. I want you to shut the fucking kid up.

LUCY. Oh. I couldn't hear you.

MR. MARMALADE. Of course you couldn't. That kid won't stop crying.

LUCY. She won't stop crying. I can't understand it. *(The baby stops crying.)* She stopped.

MR. MARMALADE. Finally. Get me a beer.

LUCY. Why don't you get one yourself?

MR. MARMALADE. Fuck you. I'm watching TV.

LUCY. It's on commercial.

MR. MARMALADE. So I'm watching the commercial. Come on, little mama. Get me a beer.

LUCY. You've had enough beer.

MR. MARMALADE. Don't give me that shit.

LUCY. This is your last one before dinner.

MR. MARMALADE. Fine.

LUCY. Do you promise?

MR. MARMALADE. I promise.

LUCY. You pinky swear?

MR. MARMALADE. I pinky swear. *(They pinky swear.)*

LUCY. If you have any more, I'm gonna call your sponsor in New Haven. *(She goes. He slaps her ass.)* Hey!

MR. MARMALADE. Shut up, you love it. *(She leaves. Mr. Marmalade was crossing his fingers when he made the pinky promise. Lucy comes back in with a beer.)* Open it. *(She opens it. Hands it to him. He drinks. She stands in the way.)* What are you doing? I'm trying to watch TV.

LUCY. Am I standing in your way?

MR. MARMALADE. You're standing right in front of the fucking TV.

LUCY. I'm sorry.

MR. MARMALADE. What are you doing?

LUCY. I'm not doing anything.

MR. MARMALADE. You're staring at me.

LUCY. I just like being near you, that's all.

MR. MARMALADE. Go away. I want to be by myself.

LUCY. Can't I just watch you?

MR. MARMALADE. No. Go away. *(He throws beer on her.)*

LUCY. I understand. I'll let you be. Everybody needs time to themselves. Call me if you need anything. *(She kisses him and leaves. There's a moments silence and then the baby starts crying.)*

MR. MARMALADE. Goddamnit!

LUCY. *(Offstage.)* I'm sorry, honey.

MR. MARMALADE. Put a muzzle on that fucking kid!

LUCY. *(Offstage.)* She'll be back asleep in a minute.

MR. MARMALADE. I can't take this shit anymore! *(Lucy enters with the crying baby.)* Shut that fucking kid up!

LUCY. She'll be asleep in a minute.

MR. MARMALADE. But then she'll be awake in another minute.

LUCY. She's just teething. This will be over in a couple of months.

MR. MARMALADE. Go back in the kitchen! I can't hear myself think.

LUCY. I'm so sorry. Just turn the television up. *(He turns the television up.)*

MR. MARMALADE. I still can't hear.

LUCY. Shhhh. Shhhh. Be quiet. Be quiet.

MR. MARMALADE. Who's idea was it to have a kid anyway?

LUCY. She'll be quiet in a second. Shhh, shhhh.

MR. MARMALADE. You should have had an abortion.

LUCY. Don't say that.

MR. MARMALADE. Why not? That kid is fucking killing me.

LUCY. It was your idea to have a big family.

MR. MARMALADE. Like hell it was.

LUCY. You said you wanted it all. A house with a white picket fence. Kids running around.

MR. MARMALADE. I never said that.

LUCY. Yes you did.

MR. MARMALADE. You're putting words in my mouth. Bradley! *(Bradley appears.)*

BRADLEY. What can I do for you, Mr. M?

MR. MARMALADE. Go upstairs and pack all my shit. I'm leaving.

BRADLEY. Yes, sir. *(Bradley goes.)*

LUCY. You can't leave!

MR. MARMALADE. I can't take this shit anymore, Lucy.

LUCY. No. You can't leave.

MR. MARMALADE. That kid is driving me crazy.

LUCY. She's just teething. Things will be better in a month or two. *(The baby stops crying.)* You see?

MR. MARMALADE. She'll be crying in like two seconds.

LUCY. I won't bother you. I won't make a sound. I promise.

MR. MARMALADE. I'm sorry.

LUCY. There must be something I can do.

MR. MARMALADE. There's nothing.

LUCY. I'll clean up more. The house will be beautiful. *(She cleans.)* You see?

MR. MARMALADE. That's not enough.

LUCY. We can go on a vacation to Mexico.

MR. MARMALADE. I don't want to go to Mexico with a crying baby.

LUCY. We can play Doctor whenever you want. Even in the afternoons the way you like it.

MR. MARMALADE. I'm sick of playing Doctor with you.

LUCY. I won't nag you about your drinking. Do you want another beer? I'll go get you another beer.

MR. MARMALADE. It's too late, Lucy.

LUCY. I'll be quiet. I'll be so quiet. You won't even know I'm alive. *(Bradley comes down with an enormous amount of suitcases and boxes. He even carries a bag in his mouth.)*

BRADLEY. *(Through a strap.)* All packed!

MR. MARMALADE. Let's go. *(The baby starts crying.)* You see? That's what I'm fucking talking about.

LUCY. Wait! Wait! I can stop the baby from crying.

MR. MARMALADE. Maybe for a second.

LUCY. No. I can stop her from crying forever. *(She runs into the kitchen.)*

MR. MARMALADE. Jesus Christ. Do you have any idea what she's talking about?

BRADLEY. *(Through strap.)* I haven't the foggiest.

MR. MARMALADE. Have you lost weight?

BRADLEY. Five pounds. I'm surprised you noticed.

MR. MARMALADE. You didn't get all anorexic on me again.

BRADLEY. Of course not.

MR. MARMALADE. Bradley!

BRADLEY. I'm counting calories. *(The baby abruptly stops crying. Lucy comes back in with blood all over her.)*

LUCY. You see? I shut her up. You can have peace and quiet. You can watch television.

MR. MARMALADE. You killed her?

LUCY. Now you don't have to leave. You can stay here. You can rest. I won't make a sound. Not one little peep.

MR. MARMALADE. Let's get the fuck out of here.

BRADLEY. Yes, sir!

LUCY. NO! *(Bradley and Mr. Marmalade disappear. She's alone.)* Don't leave me alone. I hate being alone. *(Sookie and a man enter. They are both pretty drunk. They're laughing.)*

SOOKIE. Shhh. Shhhh. *(They fall into something. Laughing.)* Lucy? What are you still doing up?

MAN. You didn't tell me you have a kid.

SOOKIE. Go wait upstairs.

MAN. You didn't tell me you had a kid. *(The man goes. Sookie sobers up.)*

SOOKIE. Where's the babysitter?

LUCY. She left. Seems like years ago.

SOOKIE. What's that on your dress? Oh my God are you bleeding?

LUCY. It's not my blood.

SOOKIE. Whose blood is it?

LUCY. The baby's. I killed her but he still left. *(She takes the blood and smells it. Licks it.)*

SOOKIE. That's not blood at all. It's only ketchup.

LUCY. Fine. It's ketchup.

SOOKIE. What are you doing pouring ketchup all over yourself?

LUCY. It was that kind of night.

SOOKIE. Is that my slip?

LUCY. Yes.

SOOKIE. You are in big trouble, young lady. You better hope that ketchup comes out or you're gonna get it.

LUCY. Okay.

SOOKIE. I'm serious. I don't know what gets into you sometimes.

LUCY. Me neither.

SOOKIE. I'm going upstairs. I am so mad at you.

LUCY. I'm sorry.

SOOKIE. You better hope that stain comes out.

LUCY. I'll hope.

SOOKIE. What?

LUCY. I said I'll hope.

SOOKIE. You better. Or you're gonna get it. *(She goes upstairs. Lucy is alone.)*

VI.

THE FINAL SCENE IN THIS PLAY
WHICH CONCERNS LUCY'S RESOLUTION WITH
MR. MARMALADE, WHICH ENDS IN DEATH,
WHICH IS WHERE ALL STORIES END IF YOU
FOLLOW THEM LONG ENOUGH

Morning. Lucy plays with two Barbies. She wears her tutu and tights. Bradley appears. Maybe Bradley is already in the room.

LUCY. Get out of here, Bradley.

BRADLEY. I know you probably don't want to see me.

LUCY. You're right.

BRADLEY. I've come with news.

LUCY. I hope Mr. M didn't send you on some peace mission because it's not going to work. I never want to see him again.

BRADLEY. He didn't, Lucy.

LUCY. Then what are you doing here?

BRADLEY. Mr. Marmalade committed suicide.

LUCY. Oh my God.

BRADLEY. I found him this morning.

LUCY. How'd he do it?

BRADLEY. Hara kari.

LUCY. When's the funeral?

BRADLEY. It was this morning. You weren't invited. He was cremated and I spread his ashes over the Hudson. And then I sang "Stairway to Heaven." Everyone said it was a beautiful service.

LUCY. It sounds nice.

BRADLEY. He left you this note. *(He reaches into his briefcase and takes out a note. He gives it to Lucy.)*

LUCY. I still can't read.

BRADLEY. I'll read it. *(Mr. Marmalade appears, not in the living room, perhaps in ceremonial kimono.)*

BRADLEY and MR. MARMALADE. Dearest Lucy, I had everything I'd ever wanted.

MR. MARMALADE. A house with a white picket fence. A new-born baby. A beautiful wife. But it didn't make me happy. So I threw it all away. And now I can't live with myself. When you think of me I hope you remember only the good things. I hope you remember Mexico, which was the happiest time of my life. Yours Forever, Mr. Marmalade. *(Mr. Marmalade commits hara kari. He disappears.)*

LUCY. Do you have a lighter?

BRADLEY. Zippo or childproof?

LUCY. Zippo. *(He reaches into his briefcase. Gives her the Zippo.)* Do you have a coffee can?

BRADLEY. I do as a matter of fact. *(He reaches back into the brief-case and takes out a coffee can. Gives it to her. Lucy lights the suicide note on fire and puts it in the coffee can.)* What are you doing?

LUCY. I'm burning it.

BRADLEY. Don't you want to keep it?

LUCY. No. I want to forget I ever knew him. *(The one-night stand man enters. He tries to sneak out.)* Good morning.

A MAN. Good morning. Sarah, right?

LUCY. Lucy.

A MAN. Right. Lucy. Sorry.

LUCY. What's your name?

A MAN. My name's Bob.

LUCY. How old are you, Bob?

A MAN. I'm 34. How old are you?

LUCY. I'm four.

A MAN. Four! That must be nice.

LUCY. It's a walk in the park.

BRADLEY. The irony!

A MAN. Wait till you're my age. Things are totally different.

LUCY. I probably won't live till I'm your age. I'm probably going to commit suicide.

BRADLEY. Don't say that, Lucy!

A MAN. Okay. Awkward. Will you tell your mom I had to go?

LUCY. Tell her yourself, Bob.

A MAN. Right. I'm just gonna go. *(He exits.)*

LUCY. Asshole.

BRADLEY. You're not going to commit suicide, are you, Lucy?

LUCY. No. I was just playing.

BRADLEY. That's a relief. I have to be going too, Lucy. It was wonderful to see you again. Keep in touch.

LUCY. Wait, Bradley.

SOOKIE. *(Offstage.)* Lucy!

LUCY. In here! Can you wait two seconds, Bradley?

BRADLEY. I suppose. *(Counting.)* One, two. Just kidding. *(Sookie enters, dressed for work. Maybe she's a waitress. That would be sad.)*

SOOKIE. Good morning. *(She kisses Lucy on the head.)*

LUCY. Good morning.

SOOKIE. Good morning, Mr. Marmalade! Is he here? Are you guys doing espresso?

LUCY. No, Mom. Mr. Marmalade is dead.

SOOKIE. Oh.

LUCY. He killed himself. He committed harey karey.

BRADLEY. *(Correct pronunciation.)* Hara kari.

LUCY. Hara kari.

SOOKIE. I'm sorry to hear that.

LUCY. Mr. Marmalade's personal assistant is here.

BRADLEY. Former personal assistant.

LUCY. Former personal assistant.

SOOKIE. Tell him hello for me.

BRADLEY. It is a pleasure to finally make your acquaintance.

SOOKIE. What smells like it's been burning?

LUCY. I burned Mr. Marmalade's suicide note.

SOOKIE. Goddamnit, Lucy. You'd better clean it up. And you'd better clean the ketchup off my slip before I get home.

LUCY. Bob had to leave.

SOOKIE. Oh. Yes. Bob is a friend from work. Which is where I have to go. Mrs. Ramirez is going to be forty-five minutes late. Can you hold down the fort until then?

LUCY. I think I can handle it.

SOOKIE. I'll see you at six tonight. *(She goes.)*

LUCY. What are you going to do now, Bradley?

BRADLEY. I haven't the foggiest. I feel like a ship lost at sea. I don't even have a reference from Mr. Marmalade. The job market is horrible with this economy. *(Sookie comes back in.)*

SOOKIE. Lucy, there's a boy outside. Says his name's Larry. Do you know a boy named Larry?

LUCY. I did a long time ago. What's he want?

SOOKIE. He was wondering if you'd like to go outside and play.

LUCY. Did he mention what he'd be playing exactly?

SOOKIE. I think he said Dodgeball.

LUCY. Dodgeball. I've never played it.

BRADLEY. It's a good game. You should play.

SOOKIE. What do you want me to tell Larry?

LUCY. Tell him I'll think about it.

SOOKIE. Okay. See you after work. Don't forget to wear your coat. It's getting nippy. *(She goes outside.)*

BRADLEY. I'd better get going, too. Start the job hunt.

LUCY. Bradley, you could stay here if you want.

BRADLEY. Really?

LUCY. Sure. I can't pay you much.

BRADLEY. What kind of benefits package do you have?

LUCY. I think it's pretty good.

BRADLEY. Dental?

LUCY. Sure.

BRADLEY. 401K?

LUCY. Yup.

BRADLEY. I can type 80 words per minute. I'm really good with schedules. And I know PowerPoint if you need to make presentations.

LUCY. That's okay. You can just live here. I don't make presentations or anything.

BRADLEY. Are you sure?

LUCY. Yes.

BRADLEY. What will I do?

LUCY. Whatever you want.

BRADLEY. Whatever I want? I don't know what I want.

LUCY. You'll figure it out as you go.

BRADLEY. Okay. It's a deal.

LUCY. Okay. *(Larry comes in carrying a yellow dodgeball. He has a black eye.)*

LARRY. Hi, Lucy.

LUCY. Hi, Larry.

LARRY. Could you give us a minute in private?

BRADLEY. Is he talking to me?

LUCY. Yes.

BRADLEY. Of course. I'll just be in the kitchen.

LUCY. Thanks, Bradley.

BRADLEY. You should put a cold steak on that black eye. *(Bradley goes into the kitchen.)*

LARRY. Last night I tried to hang myself with my belt. I was up on a chair, I had the belt wrapped around my neck. I was about to kick the chair out from under me when George comes in and he's like, "What the fuck are you doing, Larry?" and he took me down and beat me up. That's where I got this black eye.

LUCY. I'm sorry George beat you up.

LARRY. No, it was good. I was happy. Because I realized when he was beating me up that I didn't want to die. And that I wanted to come by this morning to see if you wanted to play Dodgeball but I totally understand if you don't because you've got company and all. But the thing is we can do it some other time, because —

LUCY. — I'm going to play Dodgeball with you, Larry.

LARRY. You are?

LUCY. I am.

LARRY. Cool. Okay. I'll just wait outside.

LUCY. Okay.

LARRY. Okay. See you in a minute.

LUCY. See you in a minute. *(He goes outside.)* Bradley, you can come back. *(Bradley comes back.)*

BRADLEY. He certainly was talkative, wasn't he?

LUCY. He had a lot to say.

BRADLEY. You're going to play Dodgeball with him?

LUCY. Yes.

BRADLEY. I think you're going to like it. It's a good game.

LUCY. How do I look?

BRADLEY. You look beautiful.

LUCY. Thank you, Bradley. *(Bradley helps her with her coat.)*

BRADLEY. Do you want me to stay here?

LUCY. If you would like to.

BRADLEY. I would.

LUCY. Just make yourself at home.

BRADLEY. Okay.

LUCY. So, I'll see you later.

BRADLEY. See you later. *(She goes. Bradley walks around the room. Touches the furniture. Straightens things up a bit. He takes off his shoes. Sees the La-Z-Boy. Gets on it. Pulls the lever to recline and then again to return upright. He does this a couple times, having a hoo-ha of a time. We see Lucy outside the house playing Dodgeball. She's happy. Bradley lies back as the lights slowly fade. Maybe Bradley sings during the curtain call like in* Twelfth Night.*)*

End of Play

PROPERTY LIST

Barbie and Ken dolls
Briefcase with cocaine, sex toys, pornographic magazines
Beeper, Blackberry
Bowl of popcorn
Hairbrush
Cell phone
Briefcase with heart-shaped box of chocolates and card
Calendar, pencil
Cigarette, lighter
Record player with handle
Junk food
Glasses, napkins
Trash bag, rubber gloves
Leaf blower
Moccasins
Boat of sushi
Roses, candelabras, champagne, desserts
Plane tickets
Suitcases
Beer, cigarettes
Baby in a blanket
Beer
Briefcase with note, Zippo, coffee can
Yellow ball

SOUND EFFECTS

Beeper
Doorbell
Romantic French music
Baby crying

NEW PLAYS

★ **THE EXONERATED by Jessica Blank and Erik Jensen.** Six interwoven stories paint a picture of an American criminal justice system gone horribly wrong and six brave souls who persevered to survive it. "The #1 play of the year...intense and deeply affecting..." –*NY Times.* "Riveting. Simple, honest storytelling that demands reflection." –*A.P.* "Artful and moving...pays tribute to the resilience of human hearts and minds." –*Variety.* "Stark...riveting...cunningly orchestrated." –*The New Yorker.* "Hard-hitting, powerful, and socially relevant." –*Hollywood Reporter.* [7M, 3W] ISBN: 0-8222-1946-8

★ **STRING FEVER by Jacquelyn Reingold.** Lily juggles the big issues: turning forty, artificial insemination and the elusive scientific Theory of Everything in this Off-Broadway comedy hit. "Applies the elusive rules of string theory to the conundrums of one woman's love life. Think *Sex and the City* meets *Copenhagen*." –*NY Times.* "A funny offbeat and touching look at relationships...an appealing romantic comedy populated by oddball characters." –*NY Daily News.* "Where kooky, zany, and madcap meet...whimsically winsome." –*NY Magazine.* "STRING FEVER will have audience members happily stringing along." –*TheaterMania.com.* "Reingold's language is surprising, inventive, and unique." –*nytheatre.com.* "...[a] whimsical comic voice." –*Time Out.* [3M, 3W (doubling)] ISBN: 0-8222-1952-2

★ **DEBBIE DOES DALLAS adapted by Erica Schmidt, composed by Andrew Sherman, conceived by Susan L. Schwartz.** A modern morality tale told as a comic musical of tragic proportions as the classic film is brought to the stage. "A scream! A saucy, tongue-in-cheek romp." –*The New Yorker.* "Hilarious! DEBBIE manages to have it all: beauty, brains and a great sense of humor!" –*Time Out.* "Shamelessly silly, shrewdly self-aware and proud of being naughty. Great fun!" –*NY Times.* "Racy and raucous, a lighthearted, fast-paced thoroughly engaging and hilarious send-up." –*NY Daily News.* [3M, 5W] ISBN: 0-8222-1955-7

★ **THE MYSTERY PLAYS by Roberto Aguirre-Sacasa.** Two interrelated one acts, loosely based on the tradition of the medieval mystery plays. "... stylish, spine-tingling...Mr. Aguirre-Sacasa uses standard tricks of horror stories, borrowing liberally from masters like Kafka, Lovecraft, Hitchock...But his mastery of the genre is his own...irresistible." –*NY Times.* "Undaunted by the special-effects limitations of theatre, playwright and *Marvel* comic-book writer Roberto Aguirre-Sacasa maps out some creepy twilight zones in THE MYSTERY PLAYS, an engaging, related pair of one acts...The theatre may rarely deliver shocks equivalent to, say, *Dawn of the Dead*, but Aguirre-Sacasa's work is fine compensation." –*Time Out.* [4M, 2W] ISBN: 0-8222-2038-5

★ **THE JOURNALS OF MIHAIL SEBASTIAN by David Auburn.** This epic one-man play spans eight tumultuous years and opens a uniquely personal window on the Romanian Holocaust and the Second World War. "Powerful." –*NY Times.* "[THE JOURNALS OF MIHAIL SEBASTIAN] allows us to glimpse the idiosyncratic effects of that awful history on one intelligent, pragmatic, recognizably real man..." –*NY Newsday.* [3M, 5W] ISBN: 0-8222-2006-7

★ **LIVING OUT by Lisa Loomer.** The story of the complicated relationship between a Salvadoran nanny and the Anglo lawyer she works for. "A stellar new play. Searingly funny." –*The New Yorker.* "Both generous and merciless, equally enjoyable and disturbing." –*NY Newsday.* "A bitingly funny new comedy. The plight of working mothers is explored from two pointedly contrasting perspectives in this sympathetic, sensitive new play." –*Variety.* [2M, 6W] ISBN: 0-8222-1994-8

DRAMATISTS PLAY SERVICE, INC.
440 Park Avenue South, New York, NY 10016 212-683-8960 Fax 212-213-1539
postmaster@dramatists.com www.dramatists.com

NEW PLAYS

★ **MATCH by Stephen Belber.** Mike and Lisa Davis interview a dancer and choreographer about his life, but it is soon evident that their agenda will either ruin or inspire them—and definitely change their lives forever. "Prolific laughs and ear-to-ear smiles." *–NY Magazine.* "Uproariously funny, deeply moving, enthralling theater. Stephen Belber's MATCH has great beauty and tenderness, and abounds in wit." *–NY Daily News.* "Three and a half out of four stars." *–USA Today.* "A theatrical steeplechase that leads straight from outrageous bitchery to unadorned, heartfelt emotion." *–Wall Street Journal.* [2M, 1W] ISBN: 0-8222-2020-2

★ **HANK WILLIAMS: LOST HIGHWAY by Randal Myler and Mark Harelik.** The story of the beloved and volatile country-music legend Hank Williams, featuring twenty-five of his most unforgettable songs. "[LOST HIGHWAY has] the exhilarating feeling of Williams on stage in a particular place on a particular night...serves up classic country with the edges raw and the energy hot...By the end of the play, you've traveled on a profound emotional journey: LOST HIGHWAY transports its audience and communicates the inspiring message of the beauty and richness of Williams' songs...forceful, clear-eyed, moving, impressive." *–Rolling Stone.* "...honors a very particular musical talent with care and energy... smart, sweet, poignant." *–NY Times.* [7M, 3W] ISBN: 0-8222-1985-9

★ **THE STORY by Tracey Scott Wilson.** An ambitious black newspaper reporter goes against her editor to investigate a murder and finds the *best* story...but at what cost? "A singular new voice...deeply emotional, deeply intellectual, and deeply musical..." *–The New Yorker.* "...a conscientious and absorbing new drama..." *–NY Times.* "...a riveting, tough-minded drama about race, reporting and the truth..." *–A.P.* "... a stylish, attention-holding script that ends on a chilling note that will leave viewers with much to talk about." *–Curtain Up.* [2M, 7W (doubling, flexible casting)] ISBN: 0-8222-1998-0

★ **OUR LADY OF 121st STREET by Stephen Adly Guirgis.** The body of Sister Rose, beloved Harlem nun, has been stolen, reuniting a group of life-challenged childhood friends who square off as they wait for her return. "A scorching and dark new comedy... Mr. Guirgis has one of the finest imaginations for dialogue to come along in years." *–NY Times.* "Stephen Guirgis may be the best playwright in America under forty." *–NY Magazine.* [8M, 4W] ISBN: 0-8222-1965-4

★ **HOLLYWOOD ARMS by Carrie Hamilton and Carol Burnett.** The coming-of-age story of a dreamer who manages to escape her bleak life and follow her romantic ambitions to stardom. Based on Carol Burnett's bestselling autobiography, *One More Time.* "...pure theatre and pure entertainment..." *–Talkin' Broadway.* "...a warm, fuzzy evening of theatre." *–BrodwayBeat.com.* "...chuckles and smiles of recognition or surprise flow naturally...a remarkable slice of life." *–TheatreScene.net.* [5M, 5W, 1 girl] ISBN: 0-8222-1959-X

★ **INVENTING VAN GOGH by Steven Dietz.** A haunting and hallucinatory drama about the making of art, the obsession to create and the fine line that separates truth from myth. "Like a van Gogh painting, Dietz's story is a gorgeous example of excess—one that remakes reality with broad, well-chosen brush strokes. At evening's end, we're left with the author's resounding opinions on art and artifice, and provoked by his constant query into which is greater: van Gogh's art or his violent myth." *–Phoenix New Times.* "Dietz's writing is never simple. It is always brilliant. Shaded, compressed, direct, lucid—he frames his subject with a remarkable understanding of painting as a physical experience." *–Tucson Citizen.* [4M, 1W] ISBN: 0-8222-1954-9

DRAMATISTS PLAY SERVICE, INC.
440 Park Avenue South, New York, NY 10016 212-683-8960 Fax 212-213-1539
postmaster@dramatists.com www.dramatists.com

NEW PLAYS

★ **INTIMATE APPAREL by Lynn Nottage.** The moving and lyrical story of a turn-of-the-century black seamstress whose gifted hands and sewing machine are the tools she uses to fashion her dreams from the whole cloth of her life's experiences. "…Nottage's play has a delicacy and eloquence that seem absolutely right for the time she is depicting…" –*NY Daily News*. "…thoughtful, affecting…The play offers poignant commentary on an era when the cut and color of one's dress—and of course, skin—determined whom one could and could not marry, sleep with, even talk to in public." –*Variety*. [2M, 4W] ISBN: 0-8222-2009-1

★ **BROOKLYN BOY by Donald Margulies.** A witty and insightful look at what happens to a writer when his novel hits the bestseller list. "The characters are beautifully drawn, the dialogue sparkles…" –*nytheatre.com*. "Few playwrights have the mastery to smartly investigate so much through a laugh-out-loud comedy that combines the vintage subject matter of successful writer-returning-to-ethnic-roots with the familiar mid-life crisis." –*Show Business Weekly*. [4M, 3W] ISBN: 0-8222-2074-1

★ **CROWNS by Regina Taylor.** Hats become a springboard for an exploration of black history and identity in this celebratory musical play. "Taylor pulls off a Hat Trick: She scores thrice, turning CROWNS into an artful amalgamation of oral history, fashion show, and musical theater…" –*TheatreMania.com*. "…wholly theatrical…Ms. Taylor has created a show that seems to arise out of spontaneous combustion, as if a bevy of department-store customers simultaneously decided to stage a revival meeting in the changing room." –*NY Times*. [1M, 6W (2 musicians)] ISBN: 0-8222-1963-8

★ **EXITS AND ENTRANCES by Athol Fugard.** The story of a relationship between a young playwright on the threshold of his career and an aging actor who has reached the end of his. "[Fugard] can say more with a single line than most playwrights convey in an entire script…Paraphrasing the title, it's safe to say this drama, making its memorable entrance into our consciousness, is unlikely to exit as long as a theater exists for exceptional work." –*Variety*. "A thought-provoking, elegant and engrossing new play…" –*Hollywood Reporter*. [2M] ISBN: 0-8222-2041-5

★ **BUG by Tracy Letts.** A thriller featuring a pair of star-crossed lovers in an Oklahoma City motel facing a bug invasion, paranoia, conspiracy theories and twisted psychological motives. "…obscenely exciting…top-flight craftsmanship. Buckle up and brace yourself…" –*NY Times*. "…[a] thoroughly outrageous and thoroughly entertaining play…the possibility of enemies, real and imagined, to squash has never been more theatrical." –*A.P.* [3M, 2W] ISBN: 0-8222-2016-4

★ **THOM PAIN (BASED ON NOTHING) by Will Eno.** An ordinary man muses on childhood, yearning, disappointment and loss, as he draws the audience into his last-ditch plea for empathy and enlightenment. "It's one of those treasured nights in the theater—treasured nights anywhere, for that matter—that can leave you both breathless with exhilaration and…in a puddle of tears." –*NY Times*. "Eno's words…are familiar, but proffered in a way that is constantly contradictory to our expectations. Beckett is certainly among his literary ancestors." –*nytheatre.com*. [1M] ISBN: 0-8222-2076-8

★ **THE LONG CHRISTMAS RIDE HOME by Paula Vogel.** Past, present and future collide on a snowy Christmas Eve for a troubled family of five. "…[a] lovely and hauntingly original family drama…a work that breathes so much life into the theater." –*Time Out*. "…[a] delicate visual feast…" –*NY Times*. "…brutal and lovely…the overall effect is magical." –*NY Newsday*. [3M, 3W] ISBN: 0-8222-2003-2

DRAMATISTS PLAY SERVICE, INC.
440 Park Avenue South, New York, NY 10016 212-683-8960 Fax 212-213-1539
postmaster@dramatists.com www.dramatists.com